Editor in Chief
Ina Massler Levin, M.A.

Creative Director
Karen Goldfluss, M.S. Ed.

Illustrator
Kelly McMahon

Cover Artist
Barb Lorseyedi

Art Coordinator
Renée Christine Yates

Imaging
Leonard P. Swierski

Publisher

Mary D. Smith, M.S. Ed.

Practice Makes Perfect

Nonfiction & Fiction Reading Comprehension

GRADE 3

Contributing Authors
Ruth Foster, M. Ed.
Eric Migliaccio

Teacher Created Resources, Inc.
6421 Industry Way
Westminster, CA 92683
www.teachercreated.com
ISBN: 978-1-4206-3030-5

© 2010 Teacher Created Resources, Inc.
Made in U.S.A.

Teacher Created Resources

Table of Contents

Introduction

The old adage "practice makes perfect" can really hold true for your child and his or her education. The more practice and exposure your child has with concepts being taught in school, the more success he or she is likely to find. For many parents, knowing how to help their children may be frustrating because the resources may not be readily available.

As a parent, it is also difficult to know where to focus your efforts so that the extra practice your child receives at home supports what he or she is learning in school.

This book has been written to help parents and teachers reinforce basic skills with children. *Practice Makes Perfect: Nonfiction & Fiction Reading Comprehension* gives children practice with reading and answering questions that help them fully comprehend what they have read. The inclusion of both a nonfiction article and a fictional story for each set of questions gives children practice with reading, comparing, and contrasting two related—but fundamentally different—written pieces.

The exercises in this book can be done sequentially or can be taken out of order, as needed. After reading the stories, children will answer most of the questions by filling in bubbles on the question pages. This gives them practice with answering questions in the format of many standardized tests.

The following standards or objectives will be met or reinforced by completing the practice pages included in this book. These standards or objectives are similar to the ones required by your state and school district and are appropriate for third grade:

- The student will demonstrate competence in what is read.

- The student will demonstrate competence in understanding how print is organized.

- The student will demonstrate competence in using various reading strategies to read the stories and answer the questions.

- The student will demonstrate competence in finding the story's main idea, making inferences, and making predictions.

- The student will demonstrate competence in beginning to recognize different types of reading (e.g., fiction, nonfiction)

How to Make the Most of This Book

Here are some useful ideas for making the most of this book:

- Set aside a specific place in your home to work on this book. Keep the area neat, tidy, and stocked with needed materials.

- Establish consistency by setting up a certain time of day to work on these practice pages.

- Keep all practice sessions with your child positive and constructive.

- Read aloud with your child and participate by asking the comprehension questions.

- Review the work your child has done. Pay attention to the areas in which your child has the most difficulty. Provide extra guidance and exercises in those areas.

- Allow your child to use a special writing instrument if he or she prefers. For example, colored pencils can add variety and pleasure to drill work.

Nonfiction

Mother Gorilla

It was Friday afternoon at a zoo in Chicago, Illinois. A three-year-old boy was looking at gorillas. The gorillas were in a display area. The display area was surrounded by a stone wall. The stone wall had a rail. The boy climbed up on the stone wall. He lost his balance and fell over the rail. He fell down into the display area and was knocked unconscious.

People screamed in fear. They called for help. They were afraid the gorillas would harm the boy. A mother gorilla named Binti Jua got to the boy first. Binti Jua was eight years old. Binti Jua's own baby clung to her back. Binti Jua carefully picked up the unconscious boy and began to walk with him. She carried him in her arms. Other gorillas came close. Binti Jua turned her back to the other gorillas. She protected the boy with her body.

Binti Jua walked to a door. It was a service door. Binti Jua knew this was a door where keepers could enter. Binti Jua carefully put the limp boy down. She waited until people came. She kept the boy safe.

Fiction

Gorilla Riddles

Mrs. Gray said, "Class, we have finished our gorilla lesson, and we have learned a lot. We learned that gorillas are the largest apes. We learned that they eat plants, not meat. We learned that each gorilla has a nose print. A gorilla's nose print is like our fingerprint: no two are the same.

"Class, I will now ask you three riddles about gorillas. The first riddle is, 'In what month of the year do gorillas have the most fun?' The second riddle is, 'What time is it when a gorilla sits on your watch?' The third riddle is, 'What do gorillas eat for lunch?'"

Mrs. Gray's students liked riddles. They figured out the answers. The answer to the first riddle was, "Ape-ril (April)." The answer to the second riddle was, "Time to get a new watch." The answer to the third was, "Go-rilled cheese sandwiches."

Mrs. Gray said, "Go-rilla time is over. Now it is Stop-rilla time!"

Directions: Fill in the bubble next to each correct answer.

1. **What is *not* true about gorillas?**

   (A) They eat meat.

   (B) They can be told apart.

   (C) They have a nose print.

   (D) They are the largest apes.

2. **Both stories are about**

   (A) heroes.

   (B) riddles.

   (C) lessons.

   (D) gorillas.

3. **The answer to the second riddle was "Time to get a new watch" because**

   (A) a gorilla doesn't wear a watch.

   (B) a gorilla's weight would break a watch.

   (C) a gorilla might lose its balance and fall.

   (D) a gorilla would put its nose on the watch.

4. **Look at the picture to the right. Which story does it show?**

   (A) "Mother Gorilla"

   (B) "Gorilla Riddles"

5. **Pretend you were at the zoo the day Binti Jua saved the boy. Explain how you would feel as you watched everything happen.**

   _____

   _____

   _____

   _____

A Strange Contest

Every year there is a strange contest. The contest was first held in 1996 on a college campus in Indiana. Now it is held in other places, too. What is the contest about? It is about spitting crickets! The crickets are real. They are not plastic. They are not rubber.

The contest is to see who can spit a dead cricket the farthest. The crickets are all about the same size. They are freeze-dried. Then, they are thawed for the contest. Contestants pick a cricket from a tray. The cricket must be fully intact. It cannot be missing any parts. Contestants must put the cricket all the way in their mouths. They must spit it out within 20 seconds.

When the cricket lands, it is checked. It is checked for six legs and four wings. It is checked for two antennas. If the cricket is intact, the "spit" counts. The distance the cricket was spat is measured. The winner is the person who spat the cricket the farthest.

How far can people spit crickets? Some people have spit crickets over 32 feet (9.6m)! Some contestants say the trick is to put the cricket far back in one's mouth. They say the cricket's head should face forward.

Filling a Room

A rich man held a contest. The rich man said, "The contest is to try and fill this room. The person that fills this room the most will win. The winner will get half of my money. You can fill this room with anything you want, but you must be able to carry it yourself."

Three people entered the contest. Each person went to town. The first person came back with a big sack of feathers. It was so heavy he could barely carry it. The first person spread the feathers all around, but they only covered one corner of the room.

The second person came back with an even bigger sack of straw. It was so heavy he could barely carry it. The second person spread the straw all around. The straw covered two corners of the room.

The third person came back. It looked like he wasn't carrying anything. He walked into the room. Everybody began to laugh. No one thought he could win. Then the third person reached into his pocket. He pulled out a candle and a book of matches. He lit the candle. Its light filled the entire room. The third person had carried the least, but he had won.

Directions: Fill in the bubble next to each correct answer.

1. **What do both stories have in common?**

   Ⓐ They both are about contests.

   Ⓑ They both are about what to do.

   Ⓒ They both are about people who win.

   Ⓓ They both are about spreading things.

2. **If something is intact, it**

   Ⓐ is not thawed.　　　　　　Ⓒ is not gross or yucky.

   Ⓑ is not plastic.　　　　　　Ⓓ is not missing any parts.

3. **In "Filling a Room," you can tell that the people who laughed**

   Ⓐ did not know what the man had in his pocket.

   Ⓑ did not know the candle had been freeze-dried.

   Ⓒ did not know about the cricket in the man's mouth.

   Ⓓ did not know about the book of matches on the tray.

4. **Look at the picture to the right.**
   Which story does it show?

   Ⓐ "A Strange Contest"

   Ⓑ "Filling a Room"

5. **Both contests in the stories had rules. Do you think the rules helped to make the contests fair? Tell why or why not. Use an example from the stories in your answer.**

   _____

   _____

   _____

   _____

Nonfiction

On the Third Try

Many people had tried, but no one had ever done it. Everyone had failed. Even Bertrand Piccard had failed. He had tried two times before. On March 1, 1999, Piccard was about to try to sail around the world in a hot-air balloon. It was his third try.

He was so scared, he threw up. Still, Piccard would not quit. On that March day in 1999, Piccard and his partner lifted off in a balloon that was 18 stories high. Piccard and his partner rode below the big balloon in a tiny capsule. The capsule was sealed, or closed.

The balloon went so high that ice formed on it. Over 300 pounds (135 kg) of ice formed on the balloon! Piccard and his partner had to quickly go lower. They had to get the heavy ice off . . . and fast! Piccard climbed out of the capsule's hatch, or door. Using a fire ax, he knocked off the ice.

Piccard and his partner flew without stopping. After 19 days, 21 hours, and 55 minutes, they landed. They had not failed this time. They had gone around the world!

Fiction

The Thirsty Crow

Aesop was a storyteller who lived a long time ago in Greece. All of Aesop's stories had a moral. A moral is a lesson. One of Aesop's stories was about a crow. The story goes like this:

A crow was very thirsty. The crow was so thirsty that it felt half-dead. "I need water," the crow said. "I need water soon or I will die of thirst." Just then the crow came upon a pitcher. There was a little bit of water in the pitcher. The crow put his beak into the pitcher's mouth, but he could not drink the water. He could not reach it. The water level was too low.

The crow tried to reach the water again and again. He could not. The water level was too low. Then the crow thought of something. The crow found a tiny pebble. He picked up the pebble. He dropped it into the pitcher. Over and over the crow picked up tiny pebbles. Over and over, he dropped the pebbles into the pitcher. Slowly, the level of the water rose. Finally, the water level was high enough for the crow to drink!

What is the moral of this fable? The moral is "little by little does the trick."

Directions: Fill in the bubble next to each correct answer.

1. **Both stories are about**

   (A) filling a tiny capsule.

   (B) going around the world.

   (C) being scared when one is thirsty.

   (D) trying over when the first time doesn't work.

2. **Why couldn't the crow drink the water in the pitcher when it first tried?**

   (A) The water level was too low.

   (B) The water level was too high.

   (C) There were too many pebbles in the pitcher.

   (D) The crow's beak would not fit into the pitcher's mouth.

3. **Piccard was like the thirsty crow because**

   (A) he was scared.   (C) he did not give up.

   (B) he sailed slowly.   (D) he filled a balloon.

4. **Look at the picture to the right. Which story does it show?**

   (A) "On the Third Try"

   (B) "The Thirsty Crow"

5. **Think of something you learned to do. Tell how you learned to do it. Did it take three tries to get it right? Did you learn to do it "little by little," or did you get it all at once?**

   _____

   _____

   _____

   _____

Bicycle Tires

Imagine you are riding your new bicycle. You ride over a nail, and your tire goes flat. The nail has punctured the rubber tube inside the tire. The air in the tube has leaked out of the hole. The hole will have to be patched. The patched tube will have to be refilled with air.

Imagine a boy riding a new bicycle in the year 1840. He rides over a nail, and the nail punctures the tire. The tire goes flat, but it is not air that leaks out. It is water! The tire was filled with water. In 1840, tires were not made from rubber. They were made from leather garden hoses. Leather is a material made from animal skins.

Now imagine a girl riding a new bike in 1843. Imagine her tire is punctured. This time, nothing leaks out! This is because the tire is a leather tube. The tube is wrapped in a strip of canvas. Canvas is a strong, heavy cloth. The tube is not filled with air or water. It is filled with grass or horsehair.

Now think of the year 1845 and think of someone who has just bought a new bicycle. The bike goes over a nail, and air leaks out! This is because air-filled bike tubes were invented in 1845.

Uncle Joe's Bike

Kareem was looking at his Uncle Joe's bicycle. "Uncle Joe," said Kareem, "There is something weird on your bike. The tires are very fat and thick. They are bumpy, too. Even more strange, they have screws in them!"

Uncle Joe laughed. He said, "That's because this is a mountain bike. Mountain bike tires are thicker and wider than regular street-bike tires. They have deeper and bumpier treads than regular street-bike tires. The deeper and bumpier treads give me more traction. My wheels slip less when I have more traction."

"Yes," said Kareem. "But that doesn't explain why your tires have screws in them!"

Uncle Joe said, "My mountain bike tires were altered. They were changed for a reason. They were altered so I would get even more traction.

"Why would you need even more traction?" asked Kareem.

"For racing down steep ski slopes," answered Uncle Joe. "When the screws puncture the snow, I get more traction. Sometimes I go really fast! I need all the traction I can get."

"Uncle Joe," said Kareem, "I think you should take me next time you go biking down a ski slope!"

Directions: Fill in the bubble next to each correct answer.

1. **When something is punctured**

   Ⓐ it is patched.

   Ⓑ it is air-filled.

   Ⓒ nothing leaks out.

   Ⓓ a hole is made in it.

2. **When something is altered**

   Ⓐ it is changed.

   Ⓑ it is more stable.

   Ⓒ it has more traction.

   Ⓓ it races down a ski slope.

3. **A tire made from a leather garden hose most likely**

   Ⓐ is a tire for a mountain bike.

   Ⓑ does not have a lot of traction.

   Ⓒ is best for going down a ski slope.

   Ⓓ does not leak if it is filled with water.

4. **Write what bike each tire is most likely used for:** *regular street, regular mountain, snow mountain*

   a. _____   b. _____   c. _____

5. **Do you think Uncle Joe's tires are more or less likely to become flat than tires made in the 1800s? Tell why or why not.**

   _____

   _____

   _____

   _____

Ann's Guide

Ann is blind, and she has a special guide that helps her work and get around. Ann's guide stops at curbs and then leads Ann across busy streets when it is safe. The guide touches door handles so Ann can find them. The guide gets in cars and rides on trains. The guide goes with Ann into grocery stores and on picnics. The guide picks up keys or other things Ann drops. Who is this guide? It is a horse! It is a real live miniature horse!

Ann's miniature horse guide is called Panda. Panda's coat is black and white. Like other horses, Panda has a long thick mane and tail. Unlike other horses, Panda is quite small. She only stands 29 inches (74 cm) at the shoulder. She only weighs about 120 pounds (55 kg).

Panda stays with Ann at her house. Ann is a teacher, and Panda goes with Ann to school when she is working. Panda knows where every room is in the school. Panda rings a special bell when she needs to go to the bathroom. The bell is tied to a door. When Panda rings the bell, she is taken to a special area where she can relieve herself.

Working Horse

Hello, boys and girls. My name is Toby. I am a miniature horse. I work as a guide. I work hard helping someone who cannot see.

I had a special trainer. The trainer trained me by clicking a clicker. When I did something right, she clicked the clicker and gave me food as a reward. I was never punished. My trainer taught me how to use stairs. She taught me how to get into cars. Do you know what the hardest thing she taught me was? It was not using stairs or getting into a car. It was learning how to wait. It is very hard to wait. It is very hard to stand and do nothing.

I learned how to do something hard, so I know you can learn how to do something hard, too. You must learn not to touch me without asking. It is not good manners to touch me when I am working. I am working even when I am waiting. If I am petted, I do not know if I am still working. I might think it is time to play. Then, I might have a hard time getting back to work.

Directions: Fill in the bubble next to each correct answer.

1. **Where does Ann work?**

   (A) on a train

   (B) at a picnic

   (C) at a school

   (D) at a grocery store

2. **What was the hardest thing for Toby to learn?**

   (A) how to wait

   (B) how to use stairs

   (C) how to get into a car

   (D) how to listen to a clicker

3. **A fiction story is made up. It is not a true story. "Working Horse" is fiction. You can tell the story is fiction because**

   (A) horses cannot use stairs.

   (B) horses cannot tell stories.

   (C) horses cannot get into cars.

   (D) horses cannot be trained using a clicker.

4. **Look at the picture to the right. Which story does it show?**

   (A) "Ann's Guide"

   (B) "Working Horse"

5. **Guide dogs do the same job as guide horses. Write how you think you should act around a guide dog. Tell why.**

_____

_____

_____

_____

The Top of the World

David Hempleman-Adams walked to the very top of the world. He walked to the North Pole. But the North Pole is not on land. It is in the middle of the Arctic Ocean. How could you walk there?

The Arctic Ocean is very cold. At times, parts of it are frozen solid. When David walked to the North Pole, he walked on the frozen ocean. He walked on ice.

David went with a partner. Both David and his partner used skis, and they pulled sledges. Sledges are large, heavy sleds that they used to hold their equipment. It was hard to pull the heavy sledges across the ice. This was because the ice was not one solid, smooth sheet. The ice was a bunch of broken ice floes. Some of the floes had smashed together. Others had drifted apart.

One time, David fell into the water when he was crossing from one floe to another. His partner saved him. Back on the ice, David's pants froze solid. There was no place to change clothes. There was no place to dry off. David had to keep on skiing in his frozen pants. This was so his body warmth would dry his clothes from the inside. If David had stopped, he would have died.

House of Snow

Grandpa built a house. The house was not made of wood or straw. It was not made of bricks or stones. It was not made of clay or mud. Grandpa's house was made of snow. Snow is cold, but people in Grandpa's house stayed warm. How could this be?

Grandpa built an igloo. Long ago, people in the far north built igloos. Igloos are constructed with blocks of snow. Snow is cold, but the igloos were like blankets. You use blankets to keep you warm at night. Your blankets don't make heat, but they do two things. First, the blankets keep the heat your body gives off close to you. Second, the blankets keep the cold outside air away from you.

Igloos are constructed from blocks of snow. The blocks are pressed tightly together. The blocks of snow are packed so tightly that it is hard for air to pass through them. The blocks keep inside air from leaking out. They keep outside air from getting in. People inside the igloo warm the air with their body heat. They warm the air as they cook their food. The warm air stays inside the igloo. It cannot escape through the tightly packed blocks of snow.

Directions: Fill in the bubble next to each correct answer.

1. **What is *not* true about the North Pole?**

   (A) It is on land.   (C) It is hard to walk to.

   (B) it is in a cold place.   (D) It is in the center of an ocean.

2. **From the stories, you can tell that**

   (A) our bodies keep air out.   (C) our bodies are like blankets.

   (B) our bodies give off heat.   (D) our bodies are tightly packed.

3. **Most likely people built igloos because**

   (A) they did not have any blankets.

   (B) they needed a place to dry off.

   (C) they could pull the snow on a sledge.

   (D) there was more snow than stones or wood.

4. **Look at the picture to the right. Which story does it show?**

   (A) "The Top of the World"

   (B) "House of Snow"

5. **When Hempleman-Adams went to the North Pole, he slept in a tent. Why would . . .**

   • **a tent be better than an igloo?**

   _____

   _____

   • **an igloo be better than a tent?**

   _____

   _____

Nonfiction

An African Orphanage

An orphanage is a home. It is a place where orphans live. An orphan has lost its parents. There is a special orphanage in the African country of Kenya. The orphanage is not for people. It is for baby elephants.

Sometimes elephants are killed by poachers. Poachers are people who hunt where they are not allowed. They break the law. Some poachers in Africa kill adult elephants. They kill the elephants for their ivory tusks. The poachers sell the ivory tusks for money. The baby elephants are left all alone. They do not know how to take care of themselves.

People are working hard to stop poaching. They are working hard to help the elephant orphans, too. Baby elephants eat every few minutes. At first, they need lots of milk. They only drink milk until they are two years old. Then, they start eating grass. They do not stop drinking milk until they are five.

At the orphanage, workers feed the elephants every few minutes. Workers do not care for just one baby. They switch around. This is so the babies do not get too attached to one person. This is so one day the orphans can be set free. They can go back to the wild.

Fiction

On Safari

Kim was in Kenya, hunting elephants. Kim was not hunting elephants with a gun. She was hunting elephants with a camera. She was on safari. A safari is a journey or a hunting trip.

Kim had a guide. The guide said, "You must be very careful. You must keep away from the elephants. The elephants you see are wild. They do not know you only have a camera."

Kim took many pictures. She liked seeing the elephants bathing in the water. She liked it when the elephants sprayed themselves with water. Kim's guide said, "See how they pick up water? They use their trunks. A trunk is an elephant's nose. Elephants have the longest noses. No other living animal has a longer nose."

Just then Kim saw some other elephants. Some were rolling in the mud. Others were spraying themselves. They were using their trunks to spray dust. Kim's guide said, "Elephants don't just take water baths. They take mud baths. They take dust showers. The mud and dust dries on their skin. It makes a kind of armor. This armor protects the big elephants from tiny insect bites!"

Directions: Fill in the bubble next to each correct answer.

1. **How old are elephants when they stop drinking milk?**

   Ⓐ one

   Ⓑ two

   Ⓒ four

   Ⓓ five

2. **You are most likely on safari if you**

   Ⓐ are walking through a zoo.

   Ⓑ are riding your bike to school.

   Ⓒ are driving in a fast-moving car.

   Ⓓ are taking pictures of animals in the wild.

3. **Most likely baby elephants**

   Ⓐ do not have tusks.

   Ⓑ do not have trunks.

   Ⓒ do not take mud baths.

   Ⓓ do not take dust showers.

4. **Look at the picture to the right. Which story does it show?**

   Ⓐ "An African Orphanage"

   Ⓑ "On Safari"

5. **How is hunting with a camera different than poaching? How are they the same?**

   _____

   _____

   _____

Nonfiction

Herding with Helicopters

Ask a person how a cowboy gets around. Most people answer, "horse." But there is a place where "helicopter" would be the right answer. That place is Australia.

Australia is the smallest continent on Earth, but it has some very big ranches. In Australia, ranches are called stations. Some stations are so big that it takes three or four days to travel across them. Cattle and sheep are raised on the stations. These animals roam far and wide. They go all over the station, eating dry grass and drinking water drawn from wells.

Jackaroos are boy ranch hands. Jillaroos are girl ranch hands. Jackaroos and jillaroos round up cattle and sheep. They travel far. They travel all over the station. They find the animals, and they herd the animals back to the station. The distance is great. It is too far to walk. It is even too far for a horse.

How do the jackaroos and jillaroos do their jobs? They use helicopters! They use motorbikes, too. Helicopters are used to find the animals. They are used to herd the animals. Closer to the station, ranch hands are on motorbikes. They use their motorbikes to herd the animals into large pens.

Fiction

Rules of the Road

Bessie and her brother Matt were walking along the road one day. Bessie said, "There is not a sidewalk, so we have to walk on the road. We have to be careful. We need to walk on the left-hand side of the road. This is because we are pedestrians. Pedestrians are walkers, not drivers. Drivers drive on the right-hand side of the road. Pedestrians are supposed to walk against car traffic."

The next day, Matt and Bessie were riding bikes. They rode their bikes along the road. Matt said, "There is no sidewalk, so we are riding on the road. We are being careful. We are riding on the right-hand side of the road. This is because bikes are supposed to go in the same direction as cars."

Bessie and Matt knew the rules. They knew what side of the road to walk on. They knew what side of the road to ride bikes on. Then Bessie and Matt left home. They left the United States. They went to Australia. In Australia, the rules changed! Pedestrians walked on the right. Bike riders rode on the left. Why did the rules change? In Australia, drivers do not drive on the right-hand side of the road! They drive on the left.

Directions: Fill in the bubble next to each correct answer.

1. **Motorbikes are used to herd the animals**

   (A) into pens.

   (B) far and wide.

   (C) back into the station.

   (D) that are very far away.

2. **When there is not a sidewalk, pedestrians are supposed to walk**

   (A) against car traffic.

   (B) in the same direction as car traffic.

   (C) in the same direction as bike traffic.

   (D) on the same side in the United States and Australia.

3. **If a cowboy uses a helicopter, most likely the cowboy is working on a**

   (A) small bike.

   (B) small ranch.

   (C) large station.

   (D) large continent.

4. **Look at the picture to the right. Which story does it show?**

   (A) "Herding with Helicopters"

   (B) "Rules of the Road"

5. **Why do you think pedestrians are supposed to walk against car and bike traffic?**

   _____

   _____

   _____

   _____

Nonfiction

World Wonders

There are many natural wonders. These wonders are not man-made. They are part of the natural world. Some natural wonders are so amazing that it is hard to believe they are real.

One natural wonder is a type of pine tree that grows in California. It is the oldest living tree in the world. It is so old that people have a hard time believing the tree is real. The tree is older than you. It is older than everyone you know. How old is the tree? The tree is over 4,725 years old!

Another natural wonder is a snake that lives in Asia. The snake is very long. In fact, it is the longest snake in the world. The snake is so long that people have a hard time believing the snake is real. The snake is longer than you. It is longer than everyone you know. How long does the snake grow? It can grow up to 33 feet (10 m) long. How much can the snake weigh? It can weigh up to 300 pounds (135 kg). The snake is a type of python.

Fiction

Bigger and Bigger Lies

Alejandro and Dana were having a contest. They were seeing who could tell the biggest lie. Yolanda was the judge. Yolanda would judge the lies. She would say who told the biggest lie.

Alejandro said, "When I was walking to school I saw something huge. It was enormous. It was a mouse as big as a horse!"

Dana said, "I didn't see a mouse as big as a horse. Maybe that mouse got eaten by the dog I saw. This dog was large. It was enormous. It was as big as a bus!"

Alejandro said, "I didn't see a dog as big as a bus. Maybe that dog got eaten by the spider I saw. This spider was enormous. It was gigantic. It was as big as an airplane!"

Dana said, "I didn't see a spider as big as an airplane. Maybe that spider got eaten by the dinosaur I saw. The dinosaur was really big. It was colossal. It was as big as a rocket ship!"

All of a sudden, Yolanda stood up. She said, "I believe you both. When are you going to start telling lies so I can say who is the biggest liar?"

Directions: Fill in the bubble next to each correct answer.

1. **A fact is true. A fact is not made up. What answer is a true fact and not just part of a story?**

   (A) Dana saw a dog as big as a bus.

   (B) A spider was as big as an airplane.

   (C) The oldest tree grows in California.

   (D) The longest snake is as big as a rocket ship.

2. **Which of these words from the story does not mean the same as "big"?**

   (A) enormous   (C) gigantic

   (B) amazing   (D) colossal

3. **What thing from "Bigger and Bigger Lies" is not part of the natural world?**

   (A) a bus   (C) a snake

   (B) a horse   (D) a mouse

4. **Look at the picture to the right. Which story does it show?**

   (A) "World Wonders"

   (B) "Bigger and Bigger Lies"

5. **Think of an amazing natural wonder. Tell why you know it is real and not a lie.**

   _____

   _____

   _____

   _____

Do Not Band!

Scientists band birds. When scientists catch birds, they carefully place bands on the birds' legs. The bands are small and light. They have numbers. The banded birds are then released. The bands help the scientists keep track of where the birds go. The bands also help scientists keep track of how many birds there are.

Scientists learned the hard way that some birds shouldn't be banded. Condors, for example, should not be banded. Condors are among the biggest flying birds in the world. Banding condors is very dangerous. It's so dangerous it can cause the bird to grow very ill and die. There is a reason for this.

When condors are hot, they cool themselves in a special way. They cool themselves by going to the bathroom on their legs. As their waste dries, it cools their blood. When a condor is banded, the waste collects around the band. It builds up, and it glues the band to the bird's leg.

When this happens, the condor's legs can get infected. The condor can become ill and die. Today, scientists do not use bands to track condors. They use radio tags. The radio tag is put on the condor's wing near its shoulder.

Fiction

The World Record Holder

One morning, Shing went for a walk on the rocks along the ocean shore. Shing saw something on the ground near the water. Shing got closer and saw that it was bird. The bird was caught in some fishing line. It was struggling to free itself. Shing ran and got the park ranger. "Come quickly," said Shing. "A bird is caught in some fishing line. It is struggling to free itself. I think the string needs to be cut. Please come quickly."

Shing led the park ranger to the bird. The park ranger very carefully cut away the string from the struggling bird. Before the park ranger released the bird, she did something. She looked at a band on the bird's leg. She carefully wrote down the number, the date, and where the bird was found. Only then did she let the bird go.

The park ranger told Shing, "This bird is an arctic tern. The arctic tern holds a world record. It holds the world record for how far it migrates. The bird flies from the Arctic Circle. It flies to the Antarctic Circle. It flies halfway around the world. It goes back and forth every year. No other bird migrates so far. We know this because of the band we put on its legs."

Directions: Fill in the bubble next to each correct answer.

1. **Scientists keep track of condors**

   Ⓐ by banding them.

   Ⓒ by gluing a band to its legs.

   Ⓑ by using radio tags.

   Ⓓ by cooling them in a special way.

2. **The arctic tern holds a world record**

   Ⓐ for being banded.

   Ⓒ for going back and forth.

   Ⓑ for how far it migrates.

   Ⓓ for flying to the Arctic Circle.

3. **Most likely a radio tag was not used on the arctic tern because**

   Ⓐ a band is lighter.

   Ⓑ a tern flies farther than a condor.

   Ⓒ a band does not cause the tern harm.

   Ⓓ a tern's wings are not as big as a condor's.

4. **Look at the picture to the right. Which story does it show?**

   Ⓐ "Do Not Band!"

   Ⓑ "The World Record Holder"

5. **Do you think all, some, or no birds should be banded? Explain your answer. Use examples from the stories.**

   _____

   _____

   _____

   _____

Snakebites

Rattlesnakes bite many things. For example, they bite birds and they bite rats. When the rattlesnake bites a bird, it holds on. It does not let go. But when a rattlesnake bites a rat, it does not hold on. It lets the rat go. Why does the rattlesnake do this?

A rattlesnake is a poisonous snake. It has hollow fangs. When the rattlesnake bites, its fangs sink deep into its prey. Venom is pushed through the hollow fangs. It enters the prey. If the snake's prey is a bird, the snake must hold onto the bird. This is because the bird might fly away before the venom kills it. If the rattlesnake's prey is a rat, the snake lets go. It waits for the venom to kill the rat. If the rat runs away, the snake follows it. The snake uses its tongue to pick up the rat's scent, or smell. A snake swallows its prey whole.

Rattlesnake venom is poisonous to birds and rats, but it is not poisonous to its enemy, the king snake. King snakes eat rattlesnakes. King snakes do not bite rattlesnakes, but they squeeze. They wrap themselves around a rattlesnake's body and do not let go. They hold on, squeezing hard, until the rattlesnake dies.

Stay Away, Please!

My name is Jillie. I am a rattlesnake. You humans have it all wrong. You humans are afraid of us rattlesnakes, but you should not be. We do not want to bite you. We want to bite rats and mice. We even want to bite poisonous scorpions! This is because we eat them. There would be a lot more pests around if it weren't for us rattlesnakes!

We are the only kind of snakes with rattles. The rattles are at the end of our tails. Our rattles are made out of the same material as your fingernails. You cannot tell our age by the number of segments, or parts, our rattles are made of. You can only tell how many times we have shed our skin! I can start to rattle my tail after I have shed my skin at least once. I can add up to three segments in just one year.

You should not be afraid of our rattles. You should like us because we have rattles. That is because we shake our rattles to warn you! We shake our rattles so you will stay away! You are afraid of running into us, and we are afraid of running into you!

Directions: Fill in the bubble next to each correct answer.

1. **To smell, a rattlesnake**

   Ⓐ uses its fangs.

   Ⓑ uses its venom.

   Ⓒ uses its scent.

   Ⓓ uses its tongue.

2. **Most likely, if a rattlesnake cannot shake its rattle,**

   Ⓐ it is three years old.

   Ⓑ it is only one year old.

   Ⓒ it has not shed its skin.

   Ⓓ it can warn you to stay away.

3. **To Jillie, a poisonous scorpion is something**

   Ⓐ to eat.

   Ⓑ of a human.

   Ⓒ to squeeze.

   Ⓓ to be afraid of.

4. **Complete the chart below. Show what eats what.**

   [ ] → [rattlesnakes] → [ ] [ ] [ ] [ ]

5. **Why do you think a rattlesnake would want to warn you off rather than bite you?**

   _____

   _____

   _____

   _____

Nonfiction

An Icy Bath

Joseph Medicine Crow was born on October 27, 1913. Every morning, Joseph's grandfather Yellowtail would bathe in the Little Horn River that flowed past his house. Joseph would bathe, too.

In the winter, it would snow, and ice would cover the river. Joseph's grandfather would chop holes in the ice. He would water his horses. Then, he would bathe. He would get in the hole and go under the icy water. After he got out, he would pick up Joseph and dip him in the icy water. Joseph's grandfather would hold tight to Joseph. He would not let go. This was because the current was strong. Grandfather did not want Joseph to be swept away under the ice.

Joseph and his grandfather would then walk back home in the snow. They would get very cold. Grandfather wore his hair in two braids. On very cold mornings, his wet braids would freeze! They would become stiff and hard. If hit, they might snap off! Joseph's grandfather would carefully thaw out his braids to keep them safe.

Fiction

Warm in the Snow

Dear Sara,

I am visiting Iceland. Iceland is an island. It is very cold here now. It is the winter, and snow and ice are everywhere. It is very dark, too. This is because Iceland is so close to the Arctic Circle. Icelanders are used to not seeing the sun in the winter. My friend Ulla says that in the summer there is lots of sun. She says it does not set for weeks!

You will not believe what Ulla and I did today. We went swimming outside! We went swimming in the cold and the dark. Though it was freezing outside, we did not get cold. We were nice and warm. How did we stay so warm? The water was heated. It was a hot spring.

Ulla says there are hot springs all over Iceland. A hot spring is heated by natural heat. The heat comes from inside the earth. Hot springs are heated by the same energy that makes volcanoes erupt!

Ulla and I pretended we were erupting volcanoes. We burst out of the hot water and splashed it all over the icy snow. It was fun. I wish you could have been there.

Your friend,

Tamara

Directions: Fill in the bubble next to each correct answer.

1. **Grandfather Yellowtail would hold tight to Joseph**

   Ⓐ when he would thaw out Joseph's braids.

   Ⓑ when he and Joseph would walk in the snow.

   Ⓒ when he and Joseph would water the horses.

   Ⓓ when he would dip Joseph in the icy water.

2. **Hot springs are heated by**

   Ⓐ heat from the sun.

   Ⓑ heat from inside the earth.

   Ⓒ heat from the Arctic Circle.

   Ⓓ heat from erupting volcanoes.

3. **When would Tamara's hair most likely freeze?**

   Ⓐ before she got in the hot spring in the winter.

   Ⓑ after she got out of the hot spring in the summer.

   Ⓒ after she got out of the hot spring in the winter.

   Ⓓ before she got out of the hot spring in the summer.

4. **Look at the picture to the right. Which story does it show?**

   Ⓐ "An Icy Bath"

   Ⓑ "Warm in the Snow"

5. **Do you think that Tamara and Ulla would have gone swimming in the Little Horn River in the winter? Tell why or why not.**

   _____

   _____

   _____

   _____

Floating Homes

The Uros people live on islands that float in a lake. The lake is by Peru. Peru is a country in South America. Why do these islands float? The Uros people make them that way.

First, they cut down reeds. The reeds grow in the shallow waters of the lake. After the reeds are cut, they are laid in the sun to dry. Once they are dry, they are woven into mats. The mats are bound together. They are piled on top of each other. The mats form a floating island.

The Uros people use the reeds that grow in the lake for more than their islands. They use them to construct their homes, boats, and rafts. They also burn them, using them as fuel. The reeds' soft parts are eaten like a vegetable, and the reeds' flowers are boiled to make a healing tea.

What it is like to walk on the man-made islands? The ground feels soft and spongy. Sometimes the ground gives way! The reed mats rot away. What do the Uros people do when this happens? They pile on more mats. They keep adding layers of fresh dry reeds as the old reeds rot.

Silly Stan

Stan lived in Wisconsin, where it was cold and snowy. One winter, he left cold Wisconsin and went to visit the Uros people. He visited their warm home on a floating island in a lake in South America. When Stan saw the reed houses on the island, he said, "These people are silly! Don't they know brick houses are better? Brick houses will not rot or fall down. I will make a brick house. I will show these silly people how to construct a proper house."

Stan went and got some bricks. The bricks cost a lot of money. Stan took the bricks to the island. It took many boat trips. Finally, when Stan had enough bricks, he began to build his house. It took a long time. When Stan was done, he called everyone over. He said, "This is the best house. This house will not rot. It will last a long time."

Just then, the brick house sank! It was too heavy for the floating island. It sank deep under the water. It left a hole in the island. Stan was very surprised. "Oh!" he said, "Now I understand! The best houses are not made of brick. They are made of reeds! I will go back home. I will go back to windy, snowy Wisconsin. I will show the people there how to make a light, reed house."

Practice 13 – Questions

Directions: Fill in the bubble next to each correct answer.

1. **To make an island from reeds, the reeds are first cut. Next, they are**

   Ⓐ bound together.   Ⓒ laid in the sun to dry.

   Ⓑ woven into mats.   Ⓓ piled on top of each other.

2. **Most likely the Uros people use reeds to construct their islands because**

   Ⓐ the reeds cost a lot.   Ⓒ the reeds grow in the lake.

   Ⓑ the reeds are very heavy.   Ⓓ the reeds rot in the water.

3. **What did Stan need to learn?**

   Ⓐ No proper houses are made of brick.

   Ⓑ All proper houses are made of reeds.

   Ⓒ All proper houses are constructed in the same way.

   Ⓓ Not all proper houses are constructed in the same way.

4. **Look at the picture to the right. Which story does it show?**

   Ⓐ "Floating Homes"

   Ⓑ "Silly Stan"

5. **Do you think a house made of reeds would be a proper house for Wisconsin in the winter? Tell why or why not?**

_____

_____

_____

Life in Space

Astronauts go into space. In space, something happens to the astronauts' faces. Their faces become puffy. Why do their faces become puffy? It is because of weightlessness. In space, fluids shift upward. Fluids are liquids. Our bodies are filled with fluids. The fluids inside an astronaut's body shift upward. They rise up to the face.

Early astronauts could not spice their food. They could not use salt or pepper. This was because of weightlessness. Salt and pepper were in the form of a grain. The salt and pepper grains could float away. It could make problems. It could bother the astronauts. It could float into their noses. It could float into ship parts.

Astronauts today can use salt and pepper. This is because the salt and pepper have been changed. They have been changed into a different form. They are no longer in the form of a grain. They are in the form of a liquid.

Astronauts are in space for many days. They have to sleep. Most astronauts sleep less soundly in space. They keep waking up. This is because the space shuttle circles the Earth. It circles the Earth about 16 times in 24 hours. This means that astronauts see 16 sunrises in one day! They see 16 sunsets!

Vacation on Earth

May 5, 2424

Dear Journal,

I am on vacation! We left our spaceship home. We landed on a planet. The planet is Earth. It is very strange on Earth. It is strange because things fall! Yes, it is hard to believe, but I am telling the truth. If you let go of something on Earth, it falls to the ground. It does not float. This is because of Earth's gravity. If something is lost on Earth, it is probably easy to find. This is because it just stays on the ground. It stays in one place. It does not float around the way it does on our spaceship.

June 15, 2424

Dear Journal,

I am back from vacation. I am back on our spaceship. Did you know that I shrunk on vacation? This was because of that gravity thing again. Mom says not to worry. She says I'll get my height back. This is because there is less pressure on my spine in our spaceship. This is because gravity isn't a problem here. Here, my spine can spring back to normal. Earth was fun, but it is good to be back on our spaceship home.

Directions: Fill in the bubble next to each correct answer.

1. In space, fluids

(A) do not shift.

(B) shift upward.

(C) shift sideways.

(D) shift downward.

2. Why did the person writing the journal think it would be easy to find things on Earth?

(A) On Earth, things shrink.

(B) On Earth, things moved around.

(C) On Earth, things have less pressure.

(D) On Earth, things did not float around.

3. From the stories, you can tell that you would feel weightlessness

(A) when there is little gravity.

(B) when there is a lot of fluids.

(C) when you are on the planet Earth.

(D) when you are in the form of a grain.

4. Look at the picture to the right. Which story does it show?

(A) "Life in Space"

(B) "Vacation on Earth"

Before Vacation   After Vacation

5. What do you think happens to an astronaut's height when he or she lives on the space shuttle? Tell why you think so.

_____

_____

_____

_____

The Mouse's Maid

A mouse is deep in a rain forest in Costa Rica. It is night, and the forest mouse is scampering around. It is looking for food.

There are beetles on the forest mouse. The beetles cling to the mouse's fur. They cling to the mouse's face. The beetles are riding on the mouse as it scampers through the rain forest. Does the mouse want to get rid of the beetles that are clinging on to its fur and face? Does the mouse want to get rid of the beetles that are catching a ride?

The mouse does not want to get rid of the beetles because of what the beetles are eating. They are eating fleas on the mouse! The fleas live in the mouse's fur. The beetles are helping the mouse by keeping it clean.

At the end of the night, the forest mouse goes to its burrow. It sleeps during the day. The beetles get off of the mouse. They walk all around the mouse's burrow. They eat every flea they find. They eat other bugs, too. The beetles clean the burrow as the mouse sleeps.

Fun Work

Natalie could not play. She had to rake up all the leaves. Natalie didn't want to work, but she had to do what she was told. Just then Natalie's friend Cammie came over. Cammie said, "It is too bad that you have to work. I was going to ask you to play."

Natalie smiled. She made herself look happy. She danced around with her rake. "Work?" she cried, "What makes you think raking leaves is work? This is fun! I am the luckiest girl alive! I get to rake leaves, and you don't!"

All of a sudden, Cammie wanted to rake leaves, too. "Okay," said Natalie. "I am only going to let you have fun raking leaves because you are my friend."

While Cammie was working, more of Natalie's friends came to watch. Natalie told her friends they could not rake leaves and have fun. This made Natalie's friends want to rake leaves, too. They begged her to be allowed a turn. Pretty soon all of the leaves were raked. Natalie had not worked at all, but the work was done. When her friends told her that they had fun, Natalie said, "I did, too."

Directions: Fill in the bubble next to each correct answer.

1. **The mouse does not want to get rid of the beetles that cling to it because the beetles**

   Ⓐ get off during the night.

   Ⓑ help the mouse stay clean.

   Ⓒ help the mouse look for food.

   Ⓓ get a ride through the rain forest.

2. **What did Natalie do?**

   Ⓐ She raked up the leaves.

   Ⓑ She played with her friends.

   Ⓒ She begged to be allowed a turn.

   Ⓓ She made her friends want to work.

3. **What do both stories have in common?**

   Ⓐ They are both about getting a ride.

   Ⓑ They are both about leaves in Costa Rica.

   Ⓒ They are both about one doing work for another.

   Ⓓ They are both about friends that cling or dance.

4. **Look at the picture to the right. Which story does it show?**

   Ⓐ "The Mouse's Maid"

   Ⓑ "Fun Work"

5. **Think about the beetles, the mouse, Natalie, and Cammie. Who do you think got the most and gave the least? Explain your answer.**

   _____

   _____

   _____

   _____

Just Doing His Job

Ulysses S. Grant was the 18th president of the United States. He was president from 1869 to 1877.

Presidents work hard. They work many hours. Still, presidents need some time off. They need time to relax. When Grant was president, he did would drive himself around Washington. He would drive all around the city to help him relax.

Grant would drive himself in a gig. A gig is a very light carriage. It has just two wheels, which are side-by-side. It is pulled by just one horse. One day Grant was driving his gig, and he was speeding. He was driving too fast.

A policeman saw Grant speeding and stopped him. The policeman did not know that he had stopped the president. The policeman gave Grant a speeding ticket. The fine for speeding was 25 dollars. This was a lot of money at that time!

What did Grant do when he got the ticket? He did two things. First, he paid the fine. Second, he commended the policeman in writing. When someone is commended, one is praised. One is told they did a good thing.

Running Red Lights

Mr. Swan said, "We have rules to keep us safe. For example, we have traffic rules. One rule is that one must stop at a red light. One must stop at a stop sign. This rule keeps us safe. It stops cars from crashing into each other. Police officers give tickets to people who do not obey the rules. The people who get tickets have to pay fines."

Lori said, "My neighbor runs red lights all the time. When he comes to an intersection, he does not wait his turn. He races right through. He goes through the intersection without stopping."

Mr. Swan said, "Lori, this is not good. Your neighbor should stop at red lights and stop signs. He should not race through intersections. He is going to cause accidents. Police officers are going to give him tickets. Your neighbor is going to have to pay fines."

Lori said, "Police officers give tickets to people who get in the way of my neighbor! This is because my neighbor is a firefighter. He races to fires and accidents. He races through intersections so he can help people. He puts on a siren so people know he is coming."

Directions: Fill in the bubble next to each correct answer.

1. **Grant commended the policeman because**

   (A) the policeman drove a gig.

   (B) the policeman praised the president.

   (C) the policeman gave him a ticket for speeding.

   (D) the policeman did not know he had stopped the president.

2. **Mr. Swan said, "Your neighbor should stop at red lights and stop signs." When Mr. Swan said this,**

   (A) he did not think about accidents.

   (B) he did not know what Lori's neighbor's job was.

   (C) he did not want Lori's neighbor to pay a fine.

   (D) he did not think Lori's neighbor should obey the rules.

3. **A firefighter would have to pay a speeding fine**

   (A) if he or she was speeding on M Street.

   (B) if he or she raced through an intersection.

   (C) if he or she was in a fire truck with its siren on.

   (D) if he or she was speeding when he or she wasn't working.

4. **Look at these pictures. Which one is a gig?**

   (A)   (B)   (C)   (D)

5. **Think about the police officer who gave the president a ticket. Do you think that police officer would give a ticket to Lori's neighbor? Explain your answer.**

   _____

   _____

   _____

   _____

A Big Word

The word *jumbo* means "large." It means bigger than usual. If something is jumbo-sized, it is extra large. It is huge. An elephant helped make the word "jumbo." How can this be?

P.T. Barnum owned a circus. In 1881 Barnum bought an elephant from a zoo. The elephant's name was Jumbo. Barnum bought Jumbo for his circus. Jumbo was very big. He was one of the largest elephants ever seen.

Everyone wanted to see Jumbo. They wanted to see how big he was. "He's so big!" they all said. "He's huge! He's giant! He's the biggest animal in the world!" Everyone talked about Jumbo. He became famous. Everyone knew who Jumbo was. His size had made him famous.

Pretty soon, people began to use Jumbo's name. They used it to mean something big. Instead of saying something was big, people would say it was "Jumbo." They meant it was big like Jumbo the elephant. So many people used Jumbo's name to mean "big" that it became a new word! Today, *jumbo* is a real word. It is a word that means "big."

The Artist's Donkey

Ms. Ta said, "Students, I want you to guess how the word *easel* came about. An easel is a standing frame. Artists use easels when they paint pictures. They use them to hold up their pictures when they paint. Guess how this word came about."

The students guessed that the word *easel* came from the word *easy*. They guessed this because they said using an easel makes it easier to paint.

Ms. Ta said, "Class, that was an excellent guess, but the word comes from the name of an animal! It comes from the word *donkey*!"

Ms. Ta smiled at her students. She said, "You look puzzled. Let me explain. *Ezel* is the Dutch word for donkey. In the 1600s, Dutch painters called their standing frames *ezels*. They did this for two reasons. First, they thought the frames looked somewhat like a donkey. Second, the frames carried a burden. A burden is anything that is carried. It is a load. The frames carried their pictures in the same way a donkey carries burdens or loads.

"The use of the word *ezel* spread. Pretty soon English painters used it, too. Over time, the English spelling became *easel*."

Directions: Fill in the bubble next to each correct answer.

1. **What made Jumbo so famous?**

   (A) his name

   (B) his size

   (C) his owner

   (D) his circus

2. **The word *easel* comes from**

   (A) an elephant.

   (B) a Dutch word.

   (C) the word *easy.*

   (D) an English word.

3. **The story "The Artist's Donkey" is made up. It is not a true story, but it has true facts in it. What answer is a fact and not just part of the story?**

   (A) The word *easel* comes from the word *easy.*

   (B) Ms. Ta explained that Jumbo was a real elephant.

   (C) The class thought an easel looked like a donkey.

   (D) Dutch painters called their standing frames *ezels.*

4. **Look at the picture to the right. Which story does it show?**

   (A) "A Big Word"

   (B) "The Artist's Donkey"

5. **Sometimes people will say, "Stop monkeying around!" What do people mean when they say this? Do you think an animal is behind this saying? Explain.**

   _____

   _____

   _____

What Holds You Together

You have a skeleton. It is made of 206 bones, and it protects important organs in your body. It also holds you up and helps you move. Muscles are attached to parts of your skeleton. Together, muscles and bones make your body move.

Some skeleton bones are big. Other bones are small. The biggest bone is the thigh bone in the leg. It is called the femur. The femur runs from the hip down to the knee. The smallest bone is in the ear. It is called the stirrup. It is about the size of a grain of rice.

What keeps your skeleton together? What attaches your muscles to your bones? Ligaments and tendons do. Ligaments and tendons are like tough bands. They are made of tough material. Ligament bands hold the bones in place. They run from one bone to the next, and they keep your bones from pulling or slipping apart.

Tendons are bands that connect muscles to bones. Your Achilles tendon is right behind your ankle. It connects your calf muscle to your heel bone. The Achilles tendon is the biggest and strongest tendon in the human body.

The Warrior's Weak Spot

The Greeks had many myths. A myth is a story. One myth was about a great warrior named Achilles. Achilles fought in the Trojan War. He was the bravest and handsomest warrior in the war. And he was the greatest warrior in the war, too.

Arrows would not stop Achilles. Swords would not stop Achilles. Spears would not attack Achilles. This was because Achilles was protected. He was protected by something his mother had done. When Achilles was a baby, his mother had picked him up by his heel and dipped him in the waters of the River Styx. The waters protected Achilles. They made him strong. They made it so nothing could hurt him.

Achilles had only one weak spot. His only weak spot was on his heel. It was where his mother had held him when she dipped him in the river. Achilles died when an arrow hit him right in the heel. The arrow was shot by a man, but it was guided by Apollo. Apollo was a god in Greek myths. It was Apollo who guided the arrow to Achilles' only weak spot.

Directions: Fill in the bubble next to each correct answer.

1. **A muscle is connected to a bone by**

   Ⓐ a femur.

   Ⓑ a tendon.

   Ⓒ a stirrup.

   Ⓓ a ligament.

2. **Achilles' one weak spot was on his**

   Ⓐ heel.

   Ⓑ femur.

   Ⓒ hand.

   Ⓓ face.

3. **What word did you read in both stories?**

   Ⓐ arrow

   Ⓑ Apollo

   Ⓒ attach

   Ⓓ Achilles

4. **Look at the picture to the right. Which story does it show?**

   Ⓐ "What Holds You Together"

   Ⓑ "The Warrior's Weak Spot"

5. **Do you think the Achilles tendon was named for the Achilles in the Greek myth? Tell why or why not.**

   _____

   _____

   _____

Nonfiction

Passing the Test

Jackie Cochran wanted to get her pilot's license. She had taken lessons, and she knew how to fly. All that was left was a written test. The written test was a problem. Jackie was very smart. She was a hard worker. She could fly any plane. The problem was that Jackie could barely read and write.

Jackie was born in 1912. When Jackie was little, she did not live with her real family. The people she lived with did not take good care of her. Jackie often went hungry. She was not sent to school. Jackie had worked hard to learn how to fly. She wasn't going to let her lack of education stop her.

Jackie asked to take the test orally. An oral test is a spoken test. Someone read the test to Jackie. Jackie answered out loud. Jackie passed with the highest score.

Jackie set many speed and distance records in her lifetime. She even flew faster than the speed of sound! One time, Jackie's plane caught on fire. Smoke filled the cabin. Jackie could barely see the landing strip. Jackie calmly radioed for fire trucks. She jumped out of the plane seconds before it crashed. The plane and the grass landing strip burned up, but Jackie was fine. Her calm actions had saved her.

Fiction

Dakota's Story

Marshall was babysitting his younger brother Dakota. Marshall said, "I have read you six stories. Now it is time to go to sleep. I am turning out the light."

Dakota said, "No! No! I don't want to go to sleep. I want to hear more stories. If you will not read to me I will read to myself."

Marshall did not think that Dakota could read yet. Dakota was only four. Dakota only went to preschool. Marshall said, "Dakota, one day you will learn how to read like me. For now, you will just have to go to sleep."

Dakota said, "I will read it myself. Just listen." Marshall listened. He listened as Dakota turned the pages of a book and said, "The Story of Jackie Cochran. Jackie was a little girl. She was very poor. She only went to school for two years. She started working when she was eight years old. When she grew up, she flew planes."

Marshall said, "Dakota, you are not reading. You are only saying out loud what you have heard me say many times."

Dakota said, "How do you know I'm not really reading?"

Marshall said, "Because you're holding the book upside down!"

Directions: Fill in the bubble next to each correct answer.

1. **Jackie asked to take the test orally because**

   (A) she could barely read and write.

   (B) she passed with the highest score.

   (C) she set many speed and distance records.

   (D) she flew faster than the speed of sound.

2. **What do both stories have in common?**

   (A) people who write

   (B) people who babysit

   (C) people who take tests

   (D) people who cannot read well

3. **Dakota could only say the things he did about Jackie Cochran because**

   (A) he was calm.

   (B) he knew how to read.

   (C) he had heard them orally.

   (D) he could read upside down.

4. **Look at the picture to the right. Which story does it show?**

   (A) "Passing the Test"

   (B) "Dakota's Story"

5. **Do you think it is easier to do well in this world if you can read? Tell why or why not.**

   _____

   _____

   _____

   _____

The President's Pets

Woodrow Wilson was the 28th president of the United States. He was president from 1913 to 1921. Wilson was president during World War I. People needed to save money during the war. They needed to use less.

Wilson thought of a way to save money. He thought of a way to use less. He had a flock of sheep brought to the White House. The sheep ate the grass on the White House lawn. The sheep got free food. The White House got its lawn trimmed. There was only one problem: the hungry sheep ate more than the grass! They ate all of the White House flowers, too!

People in the White House were pleased about the sheep. They were not pleased about something else. They were not pleased about a tapping noise. People were afraid the noise came from spies. They were afraid spies were tapping out secret messages about the war.

People were no longer afraid when they found out who was making the tapping noise. It was not a spy who was tapping. It was a bird! It was a woodpecker! The woodpecker was tapping on the White House's copper gutters.

Mari's Many Reminders

Mari said, "Mom, I'll get the lawn mowed. I won't forget."

Mari's Mom smiled. She said, "No, I don't think you will."

Mari put on her sweatshirt. She walked to the park. On the way, a lady walking her dog asked, "Is the mowing done?" Mari was startled. How did the lady know she should mow the lawn?

When Mari got to the park, a boy said, "Is the lawn mowing done?" Mari was startled. How did the boy know she was supposed to mow the lawn? After several more people asked Mari about the mowing, she began to get scared. How did people know she needed to mow the lawn? Was she being followed by spies?

Puzzled, Mari left the park. She went home and got the lawn mowed. She went to tell her friend Suzie about the spies. As she went in the door to Suzie's house, Suzie's father walked out. "I hope you finished mowing the lawn," he said.

When Mari nodded yes, Suzie's father said, "Then I'll take this off." He removed a paper that Mari's mother had taped to the back of Mari's sweatshirt. A message was written on the paper. It said, "Please remind me to mow the lawn."

Directions: Fill in the bubble next to each correct answer.

1. **What is *not* true of Woodrow Wilson?**

   (A) He was the 28th president.

   (B) He was afraid of spending less.

   (C) He was president from 1913 to 1921.

   (D) He was president during World War I.

2. **What do both stories have in common?**

   (A) birds

   (B) sheep

   (C) mowing

   (D) presidents

3. **What is true about the spies in the two stories?**

   (A) They were real in both of the stories.

   (B) They were real in only one of the stories.

   (C) They were not real in both of the stories.

   (D) They were not real in only one of the stories.

4. **Look at the picture to the right. Which story does it show?**

   (A) "The President's Pets"

   (B) "Mari's Many Reminders"

   Is the lawn mowing done?

5. **It does not say in the story how Mari got the lawn mowed. Do you think she got her lawn trimmed the same way that President Wilson did? Tell why or why not.**

   _____

   _____

   _____

   _____

Nonfiction

Becoming a Champion

Sasha Cohen is a champion figure skater. A figure skater is an athlete who skates, dances, and jumps on the ice. No one becomes a champion over night. One must work hard. One must practice many hours. Sasha worked hard to become a champion figure skater.

Sasha had to learn to jump on the ice. She had to learn to turn in the air while she was jumping. When Sasha was learning, she fell many times. She had lots of bruises. She was black and blue all over. Then Sasha saw another girl skating who was wearing a pair of padded shorts. Sasha thought the padded shorts were a great idea. As fast as she could, she got some for herself!

Sasha learned her jumps in steps. At first, she would land on two feet after turning. This would help lessen the falling and keep the number of bruises down. Then, she would practice landing on one foot. One time, Sasha had to practice one kind of jump many times. While practicing, Sasha's left skate blade hit the tip of her right boot many times. Sasha hit it so many times that she sliced the toe of the boot right off!

Fiction

The Speed Team

Ryan was excited. The speed skating race would soon start, and Ryan was going to skate in it. Ryan knew he wouldn't win. He just wanted to be noticed so he would be asked to join the Speed Team. Ryan knew that if he practiced with the Speed Team, he would become a faster, better skater.

As Ryan was lacing his skates, he noticed another ice skater on the bench next to him. The other skater's name was Claus. Claus was the fastest skater on the Speed Team. Ryan noticed that Claus didn't look happy. He asked Claus what was wrong.

Claus held up a broken lace. He said, "My lace is broken. I cannot skate. Don't worry about me. Hurry! Get on the ice so you don't miss the race."

Quietly, Ryan removed the lace from his own skate. He handed it to Claus. Claus was very surprised. Ryan said, "You have to skate. Your team is depending on you. I will race you another time."

With Ryan's lace, Claus easily won the race. Then, after the race, something very exciting happened. Claus invited Ryan to practice with the Speed Team! "You're going to need lots of practice," said Claus grinning, "if you ever expect to beat me!"

Directions: Fill in the bubble next to each correct answer.

1. **When Sasha jumps, she tries to**

   Ⓐ turn in the air.

   Ⓑ slice her boot toe off.

   Ⓒ always land on two feet.

   Ⓓ become a champion overnight.

2. **Ryan wanted to practice with the Speed Team so**

   Ⓐ he could skate in a race.

   Ⓑ he could become a champion.

   Ⓒ he could become a faster speed skater.

   Ⓓ he could learn how to jump on the ice.

3. **From "Becoming a Champion," you can tell that Sasha**

   Ⓐ never broke a lace.

   Ⓑ didn't practice much.

   Ⓒ liked getting bruises.

   Ⓓ noticed other skaters.

4. **Look at the picture to the right. Which story does it show?**

   Ⓐ "Becoming a Champion"

   Ⓑ "The Speed Team"

5. **Sasha wore padded shorts when she was first learning how to jump. What do you think a speed skater wears when he or she first practices skating fast? Do you think they wear padded shorts? Explain your answers.**

   _____

   _____

   _____

The Insect Solution

The police said, "We know the man is guilty. We know he did it. Now, we need to prove it." The man was sure no one could prove his guilt. This was because the crime took place far away. It took place in California. The man was in Ohio. The man said he was in Ohio when the crime took place.

The man had a new rental car. No one else had driven the car. The police said the man could have driven all night. He could have driven to California. He could have driven back. The man said he didn't. He said he had never left Ohio.

The police took the car to an entomologist. An entomologist studies insects. The entomologist worked hard. She picked out insects and insect parts from the car. It took over seven hours. Then she looked at the insects. She studied the parts. She figured out what kinds of insects they were.

What did the entomologist find? She found insects that are only found in California. This proved the man was lying. He had driven the car to California. In addition, the entomologist did not find any butterflies. Butterflies are insects that are out only in the day. The lack of butterflies meant that the car was driven at night.

The Village Flowers

Something strange was happening each night. Cows and horses were being let out. Pots were being turned over. People in the village wanted to stop the mischief. They were afraid to. This was because the mischief was being caused by a sprite. A sprite is like a little elf.

The sprite came out at night. During the day, the sprite turned into a flower. The villagers could get rid of the sprite by digging up the flower, but they did not know which flower to dig up. There were 10 flowers. The flowers were identical. They looked exactly the same. If the villagers dug up the wrong flower, the village would disappear.

One day, an old man came to the village. The people were kind to the man. They fed him. As they took him to a soft bed to sleep in, the man said, "Show me the flowers in the morning."

The old man looked at the flowers the next morning. He pointed to one and said, "Dig this one up." The flowers were identical. They looked the same. How did the man know which one to dig up? The sprite was a sprite all night. It was a flower only in the day. The sprite was the only flower without dew on it.

Directions: Fill in the bubble next to each correct answer.

1. **How did the entomologist know the rental car was driven at night?**

   (A) She found butterfly parts on it.

   (B) She did not find butterfly parts on it.

   (C) She found insects found only in California on it.

   (D) She did not find insects found only in California on it.

2. **What would happen if the people in the village dug up the wrong flower?**

   (A) The sprite would disappear. (C) The flowers would disappear.

   (B) The old man would disappear. (D) The village would disappear.

3. **Both stories are about**

   (A) insect problems. (C) identical problems.

   (B) solving problems. (D) disappearing problems.

4. **Look at the picture to the right. Which story does it show?**

   (A) "The Insect Solution"

   (B) "The Village Flowers"

5. **Why might someone who grows flowers need the help of an entomologist?**

   _____

   _____

   _____

Answer Key

Practice 1 Questions (page 5)
1. A
2. D
3. B
4. B
5. Answers will vary. Accept reasonable responses.

Practice 2 Questions (page 7)
1. A
2. D
3. A
4. A
5. Answers will vary. Accept reasonable responses.

Practice 3 Questions (page 9)
1. D
2. A
3. C
4. B
5. Answers will vary. Accept reasonable responses.

Practice 4 Questions (page 11)
1. D
2. A
3. B
4. a. regular mountain; b. regular street; c. snow mountain
5. Answers will vary. Accept reasonable responses.

Practice 5 Questions (page 13)
1. C
2. A
3. B
4. B
5. Answers will vary. Accept reasonable responses.

Practice 6 Questions (page 15)
1. A
2. B
3. D
4. A
5. Answers will vary. Accept reasonable responses.

Practice 7 Questions (page 17)
1. D
2. D
3. A
4. B
5. Answers will vary. Accept reasonable responses.

Practice 8 Questions (page 19)
1. A
2. A
3. C
4. B
5. Answers will vary. Accept reasonable responses.

Practice 9 Questions (page 21)
1. C
2. B
3. A
4. B
5. Answers will vary. Accept reasonable responses.

Practice 10 Questions (page 23)
1. B
2. B
3. C
4. B
5. Answers will vary. Accept reasonable responses.

Practice 11 Questions (page 25)
1. D
2. C
3. A
4. box on the left: king snake; other four boxes: rats, birds, mice, scorpions
5. Answers will vary. Accept reasonable responses.

Practice 12 Questions (page 27)
1. D
2. B
3. C
4. B
5. Answers will vary. Accept reasonable responses.

Practice 13 Questions (page 29)
1. C
2. C
3. D
4. B
5. Answers will vary. Accept reasonable responses.

Practice 14 Questions (page 31)
1. B
2. D
3. A
4. B
5. Answers will vary. Accept reasonable responses.

Practice 15 Questions (page 33)
1. B
2. D
3. C
4. A
5. Answers will vary. Accept reasonable responses.

Practice 16 Questions (page 35)
1. C
2. B
3. D
4. B
5. Answers will vary. Accept reasonable responses.

Practice 17 Questions (page 37)
1. B
2. B
3. D
4. B
5. Answers will vary. Accept reasonable responses.

Practice 18 Questions (page 39)
1. B
2. A
3. D
4. B
5. Answers will vary. Accept reasonable responses.

Practice 19 Questions (page 41)
1. A
2. D
3. C
4. B
5. Answers will vary. Accept reasonable responses.

Practice 20 Questions (page 43)
1. B
2. C
3. C
4. B
5. Answers will vary. Accept reasonable responses.

Practice 21 Questions (page 45)
1. A
2. C
3. D
4. A
5. Answers will vary. Accept reasonable responses.

Practice 22 Questions (page 47)
1. B
2. D
3. B
4. B
5. Answers will vary. Accept reasonable responses.